Journeys with Mary

Journeys with Mary
Apparitions of Our Lady

Written by
Zerlina DeSantis

Illustrated by
Edwin Lebel

Pauline
BOOKS & MEDIA

Boston

Library of Congress Cataloging-in-Publication Data

De Santis, Zerlina.
  Journeys with Mary : apparitions of Our Lady / written by
Zerlina De Santis ; illustrated by Edwin Lebel.— Rev. ed.
      p. cm. — (Encounter the saints series ; 9)
   ISBN 0-8198-3972-8
   1. Mary, Blessed Virgin, Saint—Apparitions and miracles—
Juvenile literature. [1. Mary, Blessed Virgin, Saint—Apparitions
and miracles. 2. Saints.] I. Lebel, Edwin ill. II. Title. III. Series.
   BT650 .D44 2001
   232.91—dc21

                                                    00-011779

"P" and PAULINE are registered trademarks of the Daughters of
St. Paul.

Published by Pauline Books & Media, 50 Saint Paul's Avenue,
Boston, MA 02130-3491. www.pauline.org

Printed in the U.S.A.

Pauline Books & Media is the publishing house of the Daughters
of St. Paul, an international congregation of women religious
serving the Church with the communications media.

4 5 6 7 8   14 13 12 11 09

Encounter the Saints Series

Saint Francis of Assisi
Gentle Revolutionary

Saint Ignatius of Loyola
For the Greater Glory of God

Saint Isaac Jogues
With Burning Heart

Saint Joan of Arc
God's Soldier

Saint John Vianney
A Priest for All People

Saint Juan Diego
And Our Lady of Guadalupe

Saint Katharine Drexel
The Total Gift

Saint Martin de Porres
Humble Healer

Saint Maximilian Kolbe
Mary's Knight

Saint Paul
The Thirteenth Apostle

Saint Pio of Pietrelcina
Rich in Love

Saint Teresa of Avila
Joyful in the Lord

Saint Thérèse of Lisieux
The Way of Love

For other children's titles on the saints,
visit our Web site: www.pauline.org.

CONTENTS

A NOTE TO THE READERS

Mary, the Mother of God, has appeared on earth many times and in many different places down through the centuries. She has been called by different titles in different parts of the world. But whenever she has come, Mary has taught us that the way for us to reach God is to follow her Son Jesus.

This book presents the stories of nine apparitions of the Blessed Virgin that have been approved by the Church. These stories demonstrate that Mary continues to watch over and protect us from heaven. Her greatest desire is to lead each of us to God.

1

OUR LADY OF MOUNT CARMEL

Palestine, the Holy Land of the Bible, has a fascinating history that dates back five thousand years. This region overlooks the Mediterranean Sea and boasts a beautiful mountain called Mount Carmel.

About eight hundred and fifty years *before* the birth of Jesus, a holy man named Elijah lived on Mount Carmel. Elijah was a hermit and a prophet who spent his days in prayer and penance.

Centuries later, when the Crusaders traveled to Palestine to recapture the Holy Land from the Saracens, they were surprised to find a group of hermits living in caves on Mount Carmel. "We're followers of Elijah," the hermits claimed. They had built a small chapel and had dedicated it to the Virgin Mary.

For many years the hermits continued their life of prayer and solitude on the mountaintop. Around the year 1145, they organized themselves into a community and began the construction of a monastery.

Saint Albert of Jerusalem later gave them a special Rule to live by, and Pope Honorius III officially approved their Rule and way of life in 1226.

When the Crusaders returned to Europe, some of the hermits of Mount Carmel returned with them. These men settled in England and France. Simon Stock, an Englishman, was impressed by the hermits' way of life. He asked to join them. Simon was accepted and then sent to the community still living on Mount Carmel in Palestine.

Time passed. The threats of the Saracens made it almost impossible for the hermits to continue their peaceful life in Palestine. Many of them, including Simon, journeyed to England. Only a few hermits stayed behind to defend their monastery.

The Saracens eventually did come to the mountain, killing the remaining hermits and destroying their monastery.

Things were difficult for the relocated hermits. It was a great change for them to move from the wilderness into the city. They missed the solitude of the mountain. They missed the inspiration they had received from living so close to God's beautiful creation. They had to adapt to a whole new way of life. On top of it all, the local residents misunderstood them and weren't always welcoming.

"Who *are* these men?" people would murmur when they saw the Brothers of Our Lady of Mount Carmel—the name the hermits went by—in town, wearing their Palestinian-type striped cloaks. "Why don't they just go back where they came from! We don't need them here!"

In the meantime, the Carmelite hermits had recognized the goodness and holiness of Simon Stock. They chose him as the superior of their order in the West.

Things only grew worse for the Carmelites. The members themselves were no longer united. Even some priests were against them and complained about them.

Simon was very troubled about the future of his Carmelite Order. On the evening of July 15, 1251, feeling sad and alone, he decided to spend the entire night on his knees praying in his room. "Blessed Virgin, Our Lady of Mount Carmel, help us!" he implored. "Please help us!"

As morning approached, a great light flooded the small room. Simon was completely bewildered. He peered into the daz-

There in the glow was the Blessed Virgin herself—Our Lady of Mount Carmel.

zling radiance. There in the glow stood the Blessed Virgin herself—Our Lady of Mount Carmel—surrounded by many angels!

The voice Simon heard was soft and kind. "Receive, my beloved son, this scapular of your Order," said the Lady as she handed him a cloth of brown wool. "It shall be to you and to all Carmelites a privilege that whoever dies clothed in this shall never suffer eternal fire. This scapular is the badge of salvation, a protection in danger and a pledge of peace and eternal union."

As suddenly as she had come, the Lady was gone. The mysterious light faded away. Tears filled Simon's eyes. Overcome with emotion, he whispered over and over again, "Thank you for your protection, dear Lady. Thank you for your love for our Order."

This vision of the Virgin Mary consoled and strengthened Simon. Shortly after, he wrote a detailed account of Mary's visit and promise. News of the vision spread quickly. Simon sent two of the Carmelites to see the Pope, and the Pope took up the cause of the Order. Soon people everywhere were asking to wear a replica of the brown scapular that Mary had given to Simon.

Today, over 700 years later, we can still obtain and wear a replica of the scapular

Mary gave to Simon. The scapular we wear is made of two small squares of brown wool fastened together by strings and worn over the neck, so that one square falls in the front and the other in the back. The scapular reminds us of our Blessed Mother's special love and protection. It's a sign and reminder that she wants to bring us closer to her son Jesus.

Carmelites traveled throughout the world encouraging devotion to our Blessed Mother under the title Our Lady of Mount Carmel. They prayed and did penance, built monasteries, and taught in universities. The Carmelite Order grew.

In 1322 Our Lady of Mount Carmel again appeared, this time to Pope John XXII in Avignon, France. She promised to bring souls in purgatory to heaven if certain conditions were fulfilled. "Our Lady has asked everyone to be holy and pure according to their vocation in life," Pope John explained. "She asked that we wear her scapular and that we pray to her every day."

We celebrate the feast of Our Lady of Mount Carmel each year on July 16, the date on which Mary appeared to Saint Simon Stock. People all over the world continue to receive blessings through wearing the scapular that was Mary's gift to Simon and the Carmelites. All agree that it's not the *symbol* that's important, but our Lady and her message. The scapular reminds us that Mary will keep her promises if we follow her requests and try to live and love according to the teachings of Jesus her Son.

She has asked so little…and promised so much!

Our Lady of Mount Carmel, pray for us!

2

OUR LADY OF GUADALUPE

It was daybreak on Saturday, December 9, 1531, ten years after Spanish conquerors, the *conquistadors*, had captured the Aztec city of Tenochtitlán (today known as Mexico City). Sadly, many of these soldiers were greedy for power and wealth and had been responsible for the merciless destruction of the native people's culture.

Just a few years earlier, twelve Spanish Franciscan priests, *padres*, as they were called, had landed nearby. These missionaries had plodded through muddy trails, climbing and cutting their way through vine-laced forests up to the heights of Tenochtitlán. They had sacrificed all that was familiar in order to bring the Good News of Jesus to the Aztec people.

The Aztecs, brilliantly dressed in their feather cloaks, had lined the streets, curiously trying to catch a glimpse of the padres. They were surprised when their Spanish conquerors, wearing fine silks and velvets, jumped from their horses to greet these ragged men.

The Franciscan padres lost no time in traveling and preaching throughout Mexico—from the magnificent cities boasting tall pyramids and riches, to the poorest of villages, where families took shelter in reed huts thatched with palms. Many of the native people soon came to love and honor these selfless missionaries.

At that time millions of Aztecs worshiped a cruel and angry god whom they believed could only by satisfied by periodic human sacrifice. Parents never knew when one of their children would be taken away to be killed and offered to the god. Young women lived in fear of being chosen to become the "bride" of this god—a fate that meant being drowned in a deep, dark pool.

The padres wanted to free the native people from this slavery of anguish and idol worship. They taught them about the one true God and presented Christianity as a new religion—one centered not on fear but on love.

Some of the Aztecs embraced this new teaching with enthusiasm. Singing Eagle was one of these. Baptized by the padres, he received the new Christian name Juan Diego. Juan Diego loved Jesus and tried to attend Mass often. As he was walking to the Church of Santiago (Saint James) in the village on that Saturday morning in 1531, he could never have imagined what was about to happen....

Approaching the hill of Tepeyac, Juan was startled by unusual sounds. He stopped and listened. *How strange*, he thought. *There have never been birds here at this time of year. It's too cold. Yet, I hear birds singing. How strange....*

Juan Diego stood perfectly still. He listened intently. The singing grew louder. It sounded like a whole choir of birds! It was fascinating. It was angelic. It was thrilling. The birds seemed to be harmonizing! Then, just as abruptly as it had begun, the sound stopped. All was still and quiet again.

Juan Diego cautiously approached the foot of the hill. He waited. He looked around.

Suddenly, he heard a young woman's voice calling to him in his native language. The voice seemed to be coming from the top of the hill. Confused and startled, yet oddly enough not afraid, the timid farmer began to climb in search of the mysterious voice.

Where is she? he wondered. Who *is she? What could she want?*

Reaching the top of the hill, Juan came face to face with a magnificent sight! There stood the most glorious Aztec maiden he had ever seen. Her clothing actually glistened. Her star-studded mantle was decorated with designs worn by Aztec queens. Her beautiful face shone like the sun. The rock upon which the young woman stood seemed covered with sparkling, precious gems. Cactus plants appeared to be emeralds with spines of pure gold. Even the dry grass and thorny tree stubs around the woman glowed with an unearthly splendor.

Juan was overwhelmed. "What's happening?" he murmured.

Gently, the young Aztec maiden spoke, "Juan, my dear one, where are you going?"

In a trembling voice, Juan answered respectfully, "I am going to Tlaltelolco, to Mass."

The beautiful young woman continued, "Juan, I am Mary, the Mother of the true God. I have come to ask you to go to the bishop of Mexico. Tell him that I wish a church to be erected on this very spot."

Juan Diego fell to his knees. "Dear Lady," he stuttered, "I promise...I will do as you have asked."

The promise was not an easy one to fulfill. Mexico City was miles away and, being poor, Juan had never been there before. But he persevered and finally arrived at the door of the bishop's house.

Bishop Juan de Zumárraga received the farmer and, through an interpreter, listened patiently to his fantastic story. The bishop sensed that Juan was a sincere and holy man, but chirping birds in the middle of winter, glittering stones on a deserted hilltop, and an Aztec maiden who claimed that she was the Mother of God were too much to take seriously.

"Thank you for sharing your story," the bishop said kindly as he ushered Juan to the door. "Come back anytime you need to talk."

Juan Diego rushed back to Tepeyac Hill. Amazingly, the radiant maiden was still there waiting for him!

Juan knelt before the beautiful vision. His eyes were sad as he raised them to meet her own. "My Lady, my Queen, I told the bishop what I had heard and seen here, but he didn't believe me. He asked me to come back to talk to him again, but I feel that he'll never believe me. Won't you send someone else in my place? I'm not important...I'm poor...he will never believe me."

"My son," the Lady responded lovingly, "*you* are the one I have chosen. Return tomorrow to the bishop. Repeat my request. I wish a church to be built on this very spot."

"I don't think the bishop will want to see me again so soon," Juan replied. "But I will go back. Then I will return to you."

The next day was Sunday. Juan Diego went to Mass. As soon as Mass was over, he again set out for Mexico City and the bishop's house. After waiting several hours, Juan was finally allowed to see Bishop Zumárraga. The bishop listened...again. He questioned the Aztec over and over. Juan's story never changed. For a fleeting moment, the bishop almost believed. Then...*No!* he told himself *It couldn't be! A choir of birds. A glorious Indian maiden. Spectacular colors in rocks and clumps of cactus. Impossible! Incredible! It just can't be!*

The bishop studied Juan with searching eyes. *But why would this poor man come so far with such a strange story? He's not educated. How could he invent something like this and insist that it's true, never once changing his story under questioning?*

"Ask Mary, the Queen of Heaven, to give you a sign so that I can know that you have truly seen her," Bishop Zumárraga said quietly.

"I will!" Juan replied excitedly. "I will ask her!"

Juan promptly returned to Mary on Tepeyac Hill and repeated the bishop's request.

The Mother of God smiled. "Juan Diego, come back at daybreak," she told him. "I will give you a sign then. You have gone through so much trouble for me. I will reward you for it."

That evening, Juan visited his elderly uncle, Juan Bernardino, and found him gravely ill. Juan stayed with him all that night. In the morning, he could see that the older man was very close to death. "Uncle, is there anything I can do for you?" Juan compassionately asked.

"My good nephew," his uncle answered feebly, "I am dying. Please go to Tlaltelolco and bring me a priest so that I can receive the sacraments. This is my only wish."

Juan felt torn. The Queen of Heaven had asked him to return for the sign he needed to convince the bishop of the truth of the vision. But his uncle, who had raised him as a father, had made a last and urgent request for a priest. What was he to do first?

Juan Diego decided to go to Tlaltelolco to call a priest. He tried to avoid the side of Tepeyac Hill on which the Virgin Mary had appeared to him, so that his mission would not be interrupted. But as he hurriedly walked past the opposite side of the hill, he looked up to see Mary stepping majestically down the slope. She approached and blocked his path.

"Juan Diego, what is the matter? Where are you going?" she asked kindly.

Juan confessed his dilemma.

"Juan Diego, am I not your Mother?" the Blessed Virgin answered. "Don't you know I will protect you? Your uncle is well as of this moment. Do not worry. Go to the hilltop. Cut and gather the flowers that are growing there. Then bring them here to me."

Juan listened respectfully. It was easier for him to believe that his uncle was well than to believe that he would find flowers growing on the frozen hill. Yet, he obeyed. When he reached the bleak summit of Tepeyac, he gasped in amazement. There were fragrant Castilian roses growing everywhere! Juan excitedly picked an armful and rushed back to the Lady. Mary rearranged the roses and Juan wrapped them carefully in his *tilma,* a type of cloak worn by the Aztec men. "This is my sign," Mary assured him. "Take the roses to the bishop. This time, I promise *he will believe.*"

Gently cradling his treasure, Juan began his brisk walk to Mexico City. Upon his arrival at the bishop's house, the doorkeepers kept him waiting for a long time before letting the bishop know that he was there.

One curious servant nudged the other. "Does he smell like roses, or am I imagining it?"

"What's he hiding under his tilma?" another asked, raising an eyebrow.

Fearing that they would send him away without allowing him to speak to Bishop Zumárraga, Juan finally showed the doorkeepers a few of the flowers. After making some unsuccessful attempts to seize the roses, the men immediately rushed to inform the bishop.

The bishop ordered that Juan be brought in to him. Juan recounted all that had happened. "I have brought you the sign you asked for," Juan concluded, "flowers from the hill. Please receive them." As the Aztec opened his tilma, the miraculous roses tumbled to the floor.

The bishop instantly fell to his knees, his tearful eyes fixed on Juan. The servants did the same.

Juan Diego was startled. *Why are they staring at me?*

The bishop and the men were not staring at Juan, but at the glorious image of Mary, with the features of an Aztec maiden, that had suddenly appeared on his tilma!

After some moments, Bishop Zumárraga rose and reverently untied the tilma from Juan's neck. He carried it to his chapel where he, Juan Diego, and all the residents of the house knelt in prayerful awe before it. The next day the tilma was taken to the cathedral. Great crowds flocked to see the miraculous image and to pray before it.

Then Juan Diego led the bishop to the very spot where Mary, the Mother of God, had asked that a church be built. The frozen hilltop was bleak. There was not a trace of color or splendor or even a single flower.

The bishop gave Juan permission to return to his uncle. Juan found Juan Bernardino smiling and completely healed. Juan Diego wanted to share his incredible experi-

A glorious image of Mary suddenly appeared on Juan's tilma!

ence with his uncle, but the older man interrupted him saying, "Juan, I know all about it! A kind and beautiful Aztec maiden visited me. She said that she had sent you on an errand. She cured me and told me to go to the bishop and witness to what had happened. The maiden said that the bishop would call her by the name the 'Ever-Virgin Holy Mary of Guadalupe.'"

The name Guadalupe held a special meaning for both the Spaniards and the Aztecs. Unknown to either Juan Diego or his uncle, this had been the name given to a small statue of Mary and Jesus found buried about 300 years before in Spain. But Guadalupe was also a significant word to the native people because it sounded like an Aztec word meaning, "the snake is dead." To the Aztecs this meant a great deal, because the god they offered human sacrifice to was a feathered snake. Mary, the Mother of the True God had destroyed the snake forever! The Mother of God under the wonderful title of "Holy Mary of Guadalupe," had come to unite two great peoples—the Aztecs and the Spaniards—into a new people, under the fatherhood of the one true God.

And what has happened to Juan Diego's tilma with its miraculous image of Our

Lady of Guadalupe? Today the tilma is enclosed in a special frame and hangs over the main altar of the great Basilica of Our Lady of Guadalupe, not far from Tepeyac Hill in Mexico. Scientists from all over the world who have examined the tilma over the years have found no way to explain its image. The tilma itself, woven from the coarse fiber of a cactus plant, should have disintegrated within twenty years. Now, over 450 years later, the cloth is still intact and the image of Mary is still bright and clear. Experts who have magnified the image and made it twenty-five times larger than the original, have also discovered the reflections of several men in Mary's eyes. Dr. Charles Wahlig, an American optometrist, has shown that the human eye reflects images like a mirror. As an experiment, he photographed his daughter's eyes, then greatly enlarged the picture. The magnified photo clearly showed reflections of the people his daughter was seeing at the time the photo was taken. In the same way, Mary's eyes on the tilma reflect the images of the men she saw in the bishop's house!

Another incredible fact is that the color of Mary's image on the tilma hasn't penetrated the threads of the actual cloth. This proves that the image was not painted onto the cloth. The experts who have examined the image of Our Lady of Guadalupe have had to conclude that it was *not* made by human hands.

Today the Basilica of Our Lady of Guadalupe is the world's most popular Marian shrine. Between fifteen to twenty *million* people visit it every year.

On July 31, 2002, in the Basilica, Pope John Paul II canonized Juan Diego. He did not become a saint simply because he had seen the Blessed Mother, but because he led a holy life. After the apparitions, St. Juan went to live near the church that housed the tilma. He took care of this special gift of Mary and told everyone who came to visit the church about our heavenly Mother.

We celebrate the feast of Our Lady of Guadalupe on December 12, the anniversary of the date on which Mary cured Juan Diego's uncle.

Our Lady of Guadalupe, pray for us!

3

OUR LADY OF THE MIRACULOUS MEDAL

Nine-year-old Catherine Labouré climbed onto a chair and reached for the small statue of the Blessed Mother sitting on the mantel of the fireplace. She pressed it to her heart. "You will be my mother," she quietly sobbed, "now that Mama is dead."

Catherine was born in 1806, in the picturesque village of Fain-les-Moutiers, France. Her childhood years weren't easy. Following her mother's death, she and her younger sister Tonine were sent to live with an aunt. After two years, their father decided that he needed them back on the farm. There was work to be done. Catherine had to help clean and cook. Her younger brother Augustus was an invalid and required constant care. And there was always plenty of washing and mending. Catherine toiled from early dawn to dusk. But no matter how hard or long her day was, she always found time for prayer.

"She never complains," one of the hired men was heard to say.

"She works so hard," another commented. "I've never seen anyone like her."

Meanwhile, Catherine had a secret desire. She wanted to dedicate her entire life to God and his people as a sister in the congregation of the Daughters of Charity, just as her older sister Marie-Louise had done.

At the age of eighteen, Catherine had a mysterious dream. In it, she was attending a Mass being celebrated by an elderly priest. At the end of Mass, the priest signaled that he wished to speak with her. But timid Catherine turned away. In her dream she next went to visit a sick neighbor. The same priest was there. As she walked away a second time, he called after her, "My daughter, you turn from me now, but one day you will be glad to come with me. God has plans for you."

Catherine often spoke of her vocation, but her father opposed it. "No! I've already given one daughter to God," he cried. "I won't allow you to go."

Catherine waited a few more months and tried again. "Please, Father, give me permission to enter the convent."

"I don't want to hear another word of it," Mr. Labouré answered gruffly. "I'll never give you my permission. Besides, there's plenty of work to be done right here!"

Catherine obeyed. But her desire to give herself to God continued to grow stronger. Years passed. Catherine matured into a lovely young woman. Hoping to take her mind off the convent, her father sent her to Paris to work as a waitress in the café owned by her brother Charles. After a miserable year there, her brothers and sisters managed to help Catherine escape to the town of Châtillon. Hubert, another one of her brothers, and his wife Jeanne lived in Châtillon. Catherine was thrilled to learn that the Daughters of Charity had a convent and hospital there, and she went to visit the sisters. In the parlor she recognized a painting of the priest she had seen in her dream. "Who is this priest?" she asked.

"That's Saint Vincent de Paul, the founder of our congregation," one of the sisters explained.

Now Catherine was absolutely sure that God wanted her to be a Daughter of Charity.

She approached her father again. "All right. You can enter the convent," he snapped. "But they'll never accept you without a dowry, and I won't provide one. Go ahead, join them...if they'll take you!"

At that time it was the custom for a young woman entering religious life to bring with her a dowry—the money and personal things she would need for life in the convent. Catherine had no money of her own, but to her surprise, Hubert and Jeanne offered to give her everything she needed.

Catherine was overjoyed. But there was another obstacle she hadn't counted on. She found the superior of the Daughters of Charity unwilling to accept her because of her lack of education. This time one of the sisters themselves came to her rescue. "Mother," Sister Victoire pleaded, "remember that Saint Vincent loved simple and innocent peasants. Please give Catherine a chance." The superior finally gave in and Catherine entered the convent in Châtillon on January 22, 1830. She was twenty-three years old.

After three months of training as a postulant, Catherine was transferred to the sisters' novitiate in Paris. The body of Saint Vincent de Paul had just been brought to the new church of the Vincentian Fathers there, and prayers of gratitude were being offered for several nights at the church. Three times after coming home from the church with the other sisters, Catherine saw a vision of Saint Vincent's heart. This was just the beginning of the extraordinary things that would happen to this very ordinary sister....

During the nine months of her novitiate, Catherine was also allowed to see Jesus, truly present in the Holy Eucharist, each time she entered the chapel.

On the evening before the feast of Saint Vincent de Paul, July 18, 1830, Sister Catherine was awakened by a voice calling, "Sister...Sister...Sister!"

Opening her eyes, she saw a child, dressed in white standing beside her bed. He appeared to be four or five years old. "Hurry! Get up and come to the chapel," he excitedly invited her. "The Blessed Virgin is waiting for you!"

Catherine looked around, wondering if any of the other sisters would hear her.

Answering her unspoken thought, the child quickly added, "Don't worry. It's 11:30. Everyone is asleep."

Catherine slipped out of bed and quickly dressed. She followed her mysterious visitor—who was surrounded by a glow of light—down to the chapel. Amazingly, wherever they went, all the lights were lit. When they arrived at the chapel, the heavy wooden door opened by itself at the touch of the little child's fingertip.

The chapel was bright with light. All the candles were burning. The child brought Sister Catherine to the sanctuary, to the side of a chair. Finally the little boy announced, "Here is the Blessed Virgin."

Catherine heard something that sounded like the rustling of silk. She glanced in the direction of the sound and saw a Lady taking a seat in the chair on the steps leading to the altar.

Could this really be the Blessed Mother? she wondered.

As soon as this doubt came into her mind, the child spoke again, but this time sternly and in the voice of a grown man: "This *is* the Blessed Virgin!"

Magnetically drawn to her, Sister Catherine dropped to her knees before the Lady and rested her toil-worn hands in Mary's lap. "It was the most beautiful moment of my life," Catherine later remembered. The young novice stayed there for two wonderful hours speaking with the Blessed Mother. She didn't want the visit to *ever* end. But, finally, Mary faded away. "She is gone now," observed the young child, who had remained there the whole time. Catherine followed the boy back to her room. There he vanished as mysteriously as he had come—in a ball of light. Sister Catherine was convinced that he was her guardian angel, to whom she had so often prayed.

Catherine climbed back into bed. She heard the clock chime twice. It was two o'clock in the morning. She closed her eyes and tried to sleep. But she couldn't. She was just too excited.

Mary's words kept running through her mind: "Sorrow will come to France, and the throne will be overturned…. Come to the foot of the altar to pray in times of trouble. Here, graces will be given to all those who ask for them with confidence…. Pray…. You have a mission to fulfill."

But what is this mission? Sister Catherine wondered. *The Blessed Mother didn't say.*

The next day, Catherine went back to her duties as if nothing had happened. She told no one about the Blessed Virgin's visit.

Mary's plea kept coming back to her as she worked, "Come to the foot of the altar. Pray."

On November 27, when Catherine was praying in the chapel with the other sisters, she again heard a sound like the rustling of silk. Turning toward it, she saw Mary, clothed in a white dress that was as radiant as the sun, and standing on a white globe. A snake was coiled around the globe. The Blessed Virgin's face was indescribably beautiful. In her hands she held a golden ball topped with a small cross. Catherine gazed in wonder at the magnificent sight. Suddenly, her attention was drawn to Mary's fingers. The Blessed Mother was wearing rings—three on each finger. Each ring was set with gems. Some were more beautiful than others. Rays of dazzling light were coming from each of the rings. This light was so bright that Sister Catherine could no longer see the feet of the Lady. Then Mary lowered her eyes to look at Catherine. "This ball represents the whole world, especially France, and each person in particular," the Blessed Mother explained. "These rays of light stand for the graces I give to those who ask for them."

By this time, Catherine was so over-whelmed that she had even forgotten where she was. Then, all at once, an oval frame formed around Mary. Inside the frame, these words written in gold appeared: "O Mary, conceived without sin, pray for us who have recourse to you." The golden ball disappeared in the overpowering burst of light. Then the Blessed Mother stretched out her hands at her side as the rays of light continued to pour from her rings. "Have a medal made after the model you see here," Mary instructed. "All who wear it with confidence will receive great graces. They should wear it around the neck."

Just then, the vision appeared to turn. Sister Catherine saw on the reverse side a large "M" positioned beneath a bar with a cross over it, a symbol of Mary at the foot of Jesus' cross. Below this was the heart of Jesus crowned with thorns and the heart of Mary pierced by a sword. Circling these images were twelve stars, which can be seen as a reference to the text from the Book of Revelation: "A great sign appeared in the sky, a woman clothed with the sun, with the moon under her feet, and on her head a crown of twelve stars" (Rv 12:1).

As the young sister watched in awe, the entire vision disappeared, "like a candle that's blown out," she later said.

My mission! Catherine reflected. *This is my mission! Somehow, somewhere, I must have someone make medals patterned after this vision, just as Mary has asked.* Sister Catherine also understood that she herself should remain unknown. She was to be Mary's hidden messenger.

During the next forty-six years, in obedience to the Blessed Mother, the only person to whom Sister Catherine revealed her mission was Father Aladel, her confessor. Catherine quietly continued her duties as cook, laundress and housekeeper with humble love and dedication.

The first medals were made in 1832, with the permission of the Archbishop of Paris. In a short time, so many graces were received by people who wore it and prayed to Mary that it spontaneously came to be called the "Miraculous Medal." This is the name by which it is still known today.

Most of her fellow sisters never suspected that Catherine was the sister who had seen the Blessed Virgin. Whenever someone tried to guess and attention was turned to her, Sister Catherine had a way of ingeniously changing the subject.

For forty years, Sister Catherine was assigned to work in a home for the elderly near Paris. She was in charge of the men's wing and gave the sick and aged men constant and devoted care.

But something was still bothering her. In one of her visions, the Blessed Mother had asked that Sister Catherine have a statue made showing Mary presenting the globe of the earth to God. Father Aladel had died. No one else knew that Mary had visited Catherine. Who would help her to get the statue made? Catherine sensed that her life was drawing to a close. She worried about dying without having completed the entire mission the Blessed Virgin had entrusted to her. *I must reveal my identity now,* she decided, *I must, in order to see the statue completed before I die.*

After asking Mary's permission, Catherine finally went to her superior, Sister Jeanne Dufès, and told her everything.

"You've received a great blessing," concluded Sister Jeanne.

"I've only been God's instrument," Sister Catherine quietly replied. "I'm not well educated. If the Blessed Mother chose me, it was only to show that everything came from her."

The statue was finally begun. Sister Catherine got to see the plaster mold before she died. But she was disappointed with it. "The Blessed Mother is much more beautiful!" she exclaimed.

Sister Catherine Labouré died on December 31, 1876. Pope Pius XII declared her a saint in 1947. Today Catherine's incorrupt body rests beneath an altar that was built on the very spot where the Blessed Mother appeared to her. Over this altar is the statue of Our Lady of the Globe. Each year a million pilgrims visit the chapel in Paris, France, where Mary appeared to Catherine. The feast of Our Lady of the Miraculous Medal is celebrated there on November 27.

Today the Miraculous Medal continues to remind each of us of Mary's love and care, and also of her message: "Come to the foot of the altar. Pray!"

Our Lady of the Miraculous Medal, pray for us!

4

OUR LADY OF LA SALETTE

Fifteen-year-old Melanie Mathieu was a quiet girl and a conscientious worker. Through no fault of her own, she had never attended school, and had had very little instruction in her Catholic faith. Melanie had been obliged, since the age of seven, to find odd jobs to help her family. And it certainly was a challenge to find work in Corps, a tiny, isolated village deep in the French Alps.

Fortunately, Jean Baptiste Pra, one of the local farmers, had now hired Melanie to tend his small herd of cows. She earned very little, but with seven other children in the family, her parents were grateful for every extra penny.

Eleven-year-old Maximin Giraud was also from Corps. Unlike Melanie, Maximin didn't take work too seriously. His birth mother had died and his father had remarried. Unfortunately, Maximin didn't get along well with his stepmother. To add to the boy's problems, his father often drank too much.

Although Corps had a population of only 1,000, Maximin and Melanie had never met. Not until September 1846....

Pierre Selme owned four cows that had to be pastured in a meadow alongside Mr. Pra's land. One day Mr. Selme's usual herder became ill. "Could Maximin possibly fill in for a week?" he asked Mr. Giraud, Maximin's father.

"Why not?" Mr. Giraud replied.

On Thursday, September 17, Maximin and Melanie met as they drove their cows out to the meadow. Even though Melanie was shy, it could be very lonely in mountains. For his part, Maximin, with his outgoing personality, was happy to discover a companion in the fields. The two began talking and had lunch together. They got together again on Friday. And again on Saturday, September 19.

By noon on Saturday, the young herders had rounded up their charges and led them to a nearby ravine to water them. This accomplished, they pulled out their meager supply of bread and cheese and settled down for lunch. After the quick meal, the two stretched out on the carpet of fresh, green grass for a short nap.

It was such a beautiful day. The breeze

brushed softly against their cheeks. The sun warmed them. Soon they were fast asleep....

Melanie was the first to awaken. "Maximin, wake up, wake up!" she cried in alarm. "We overslept! I can't see the cows!"

The sleeping boy opened his eyes and jumped to his feet.

"Don't worry," he reassured, "we'll find them."

The two split up to search for their charges. Soon Maximin let out a triumphant shout, "There they are, Melanie! Over on the hillside! They're all there."

As a grateful Melanie began to gather up their knapsacks, she suddenly became conscious of a bright circle of light hovering in the ravine.

Could it be the sun? she wondered. *No, no...it's brighter than the sun and more dazzling.* Shading her eyes with both hands she gazed at the unusual, brilliant sphere of light.

She tried to call Maximin several times, but the words caught in her throat. Finally she managed to gasp "Maximin...look....quick!"

Maximin spun around. He stared in amazement at what he saw. "What is it?" he half whispered.

"I don't know, I don't know, Maximin.

Let's get out of here!" Melanie cried, tugging at her friend's sleeve.

But in a fleeting moment before either could utter another syllable, the bright circle of light began to spread apart before their very eyes. The children stood petrified and motionless, as if rooted to the ground.

"Look!" Melanie's voice cracked with fear. "There's a Lady in the light! Do you see her?"

"You're right," the boy replied in awe. "There *is* a Lady in the light. She's moving now. She's going to sit down."

"Why is she covering her face with her hands?" Melanie asked in a shaky voice. "Who can she be?"

"I don't know," Maximin shot back. "But let's get out of here!"

"No, wait," Melanie pleaded. "Such a lovely Lady couldn't possibly hurt us. Wait. Let's watch."

"No! Let's go!"

"She's getting up. She's crossing her hands on her breast. She looks so sad."

The children's fear was slowly being overcome by their astonishment.

"She's wearing such a big golden cross around her neck," Maximin observed.

The friends huddled close to each other.

Cautiously they took a few steps closer toward the vision. As they stared, both noticed tears running down the Lady's cheeks.

"She's crying," Melanie announced, suddenly moved with deep emotion.

"What would someone so beautiful have to cry about?" Maximin wondered aloud.

"I think she's going to speak to us. Be quiet. Listen."

"Come to me, my children," they heard the Lady say. "Do not be afraid. I have something very important to tell you."

As if in a dream, the children drew closer until they seemed to be within touching distance of the beautiful Lady.

"The people of France have been using my Son's name in vain so frequently lately," the Lady continued. "Their curses offend my Son. And they do not observe Sunday as my Son asked. They are moving farther and farther away from him. He is so saddened by the sins of humanity. If this continues, there will be a famine in France. This will not happen if the people will return to my Son." The Lady paused. Then she asked, "Do you say your prayers well, my children?"

Lowering their heads, the two admitted that they often forgot to pray.

"It is very important that you say your

*"My children, I have come to beg
all my people to pray to my Son."*

prayers at night and in the morning," the Lady responded. "When you don't have time, at least say an Our Father and a Hail Mary. And when you can, say more. My children, you will make it known to all my people that I have come to beg them to pray to my Son."

Then slowly the Lady began moving away. As she glided over the ravine, without turning back, the children heard her repeat again, "You will make this known to all my people." Then she rose up into the air.

"She seems to be floating over the world, looking down on all the people," Melanie whispered.

Gradually, the radiant light again enfolded the beautiful Lady. Then both the Lady and the light slowly faded into the air.

Maximin took a deep breath. "I wonder who she was," he thought aloud.

"Maybe she was a great saint," a confused Melanie answered.

The two stood still for a few moments, letting their eyes wander over the ravine. Everything looked just as it always had.

"She's gone," Melanie sighed in disappointment.

"She was so beautiful," Maximin murmured, still gazing into the distance.

"And so sad," Melanie added.

There was nothing left to do but go back to their cows. They did. But they couldn't stop thinking about the strange happening.

Later that afternoon, when they returned the herds to their owners, Maximin revealed the whole story to Pierre Selme. Mr. Selme was uneasy about the tale. After supper, he brought Maximin to Jean Baptiste Pra's house. He learned from Mr. Pra that Melanie had said nothing about the children's afternoon adventure. Maximin repeated his story to the Pra family. When Melanie was called in from the stable and questioned, her version of the story perfectly matched Maximin's.

"Maybe you should tell the priest at La Salette about this," Mr. Pra finally suggested.

The following morning, the two children obediently set out for the rectory. The pastor received them kindly. Tears filled his eyes as he listened to their story.

"I believe you," the priest said quietly when they finished. "The Lady whom you saw must have been the Blessed Virgin."

Melanie and Maximin looked at each other in great surprise.

The Blessed Mother's message spread quickly throughout the surrounding villages. The peasants knew only too well that that words uttered by the children were divinely inspired. They knew only too well the truth behind the message. They *had* let God slip out of their lives. They *had* saddened the Blessed Virgin. They *did* need to change their lives.

Maximin and Melanie saw each other only occasionally after that, but families throughout the region took Mary's message to heart and began to pray, to stop cursing and to keep Sundays holy by going to Mass and avoiding all unnecessary work.

A basilica was eventually built on the site of Mary's apparition at La Salette, and people from all over the world began to visit and pray there. Many who came felt themselves drawn to be reconciled to God, and, after receiving the sacrament of Penance, found new peace in living according to the teachings of Jesus. The feast of Our Lady of La Salette is celebrated at the shrine each year on September 19.

Today, the message of Our Lady of La Salette remains as important for us as it was for the people living in 1846: "Pray to my Son Jesus! Do not use his name in the wrong way! Keep Sundays holy!"

Our Lady of La Salette, pray for us!

5

OUR LADY OF LOURDES

"The wood's all gone," fourteen-year-old Bernadette reported as she straightened up from the fireplace.

A fire was essential to ward off the damp February chill that held the Soubirous family's one-room home—a former prison—in its icy grip.

"Look, here comes Jeanne," Bernadette's younger sister Toinette announced, pointing out the window. "She'll come with us to gather more wood."

Mrs. Soubirous turned to Bernadette. "It's drizzling out. It will be very bad for your asthma—"

"I'll wear my cloak and hood, Mama," Bernadette broke in. "Please let me go."

"All right," Mrs. Soubirous sighed. "But be sure not to get your feet wet."

"I won't," Bernadette promised. Slipping on her *sabots*—wooden clogs—she ran out to join Toinette and her friend Jeanne.

The three quickly made their way to a spot called Massabielle. There at the bottom of a cliff was a grotto, a kind of natural cave carved out of the rock. Scattered around the grotto the girls could see fallen branches that would make good firewood. The only problem was that a small stream branching off from the Gave River ran between them and the grotto. Jeanne wasn't going to let that stop her. She kicked off her sabots and started wading through the frigid water. "Come on, Toinette!" she called.

Toinette squealed loudly as she hopped across the shallow stream.

Bernadette knew she shouldn't risk a wade to the other side. "Toinette!" she cried, "Help me to throw some big stones in so that I can walk across."

"Maybe I could carry you," her sister shouted back.

"No. You're too small. But I think Jeanne is strong enough."

"Stay where you are if you can't cross over!" Jeanne impatiently yelled.

As the two girls moved off to search for more wood, Bernadette was left alone. She removed her sabots. Just as she was taking off her first stocking in an attempt to cross the stream, she heard a loud rumble. She looked around. There were no signs of an approaching storm. She bent again. Again came the loud noise. Bernadette stood and scanned the area in every direction. A sudden movement caught her eye. Above the grotto in a smaller hollow of the cliff, a wild rosebush was tossing wildly, as if caught in a storm. All the other trees were perfectly still.

As she watched, a cloud of light filled the hollow behind the rosebush. Within the light appeared a beautiful young woman. She seemed to be about sixteen or seventeen years old. She wore a long white dress with a blue sash at the waist, and a white veil, which almost touched the ground. A yellow rose rested on each of her bare feet. The Lady smiled in welcome. Bernadette fell to her knees. Not realizing what she was doing, she pulled her rosary from her pocket and tried to make the sign of the cross. To her amazement, Bernadette found that she couldn't raise her hand. *What was happening?* The Lady was now making the sign of the cross. After she had finished, Bernadette was able to sign herself. The young Lady passed the beads of her own white rosary through her fingers as Bernadette prayed the rosary. But Bernadette noticed that she silently moved her lips only at the "Glory be to the Father, and to the Son, and to the Holy Spirit" at the following each decade. As

Bernadette finished the rosary, the smiling young Lady stepped back into the niche. In a moment or two she was gone, and the brilliant light had faded away.

When Toinette and Jeanne returned on the opposite side of the stream, they saw Bernadette kneeling.

"Are you coming to help us or not?" Jeanne shouted.

"Yes, I'm coming!" Bernadette replied. Hurriedly pulling off her second stocking, she quickly crossed the stream, feeling no cold at all.

After having collected a good supply of branches, the three girls prepared to leave for home.

"Toinette, did you see anything at the grotto?" Bernadette casually asked as she tied her bundle of wood.

"No. Why?"

"I was just wondering," Bernadette quickly answered. "We'd better go now."

Jeanne ran on ahead while the two sisters walked together.

Bernadette's acting strangely, thought Toinette. "What did *you* see back there, Bernadette?" she suddenly burst out.

"Do you promise to keep it a secret?"

"Yes!" the eleven-year-old practically shouted.

The words came rushing out and in a few minutes Bernadette had revealed everything to her sister.

At first Toinette felt frightened. But as they walked on, her fear turned to anger and jealousy. *Who does Bernadette think she is? It's bad enough that she always gets special treatment because she's sick. But now she's making up things. Mama should know about this!*

They had only been in the house a few minutes when Toinette broke her promise and told the whole secret to their mother.

"You mustn't go back there again, Bernadette!" Mrs. Soubirous said sternly. "And get these crazy ideas out of your head."

Bernadette had a hard time sleeping that night. The next day, Friday, she felt impelled to return to the grotto, but her mother refused to allow it. By Sunday the urge to return to Massabielle was overpowering. "Please let me go back, Mama," Bernadette pleaded.

"Only if your father gives you permission," Mrs. Soubirous answered gruffly.

Bernadette managed to get her father to

agree, and soon she was running toward Massabielle trailed by Toinette, Jeanne, and some of their other friends. At the grotto she fell to her knees exactly where she had knelt the first day. "She's there!" she excitedly exclaimed. One of the girls handed Bernadette the bottle of holy water they had brought along. Bernadette sprinkled some in the direction of the Lady. "If you are from God, come forward!" she cried. The beautiful young Lady obligingly moved up to the edge of the niche!

Bernadette's face had taken on a heavenly expression and her eyes were fixed on the grotto. When the girls tried to talk to her and get her to stand, she neither heard nor moved. She had to be carried away that day by Antoine Nicolau, a local miller.

In the days that followed, the entire town of Lourdes was buzzing with news of the strange happenings at Massabielle. Bernadette's parents had forbidden her to return there. But again Bernadette felt irresistibly drawn to the spot. When a wealthy lady whom Bernadette's mother worked for, asked Mrs. Soubirous to allow Bernadette to accompany her and her friend to the grotto, Mrs. Soubirous felt she couldn't refuse.

Early on the morning of Thursday, February 18, while it was still dark out, Bernadette and the two women headed for Massabielle. Once again the beautiful Lady appeared in the hollow of the rock. This time Bernadette offered her a pen and paper and asked her to write down her name and what she wished. For the first time the Lady spoke. "It is not necessary for me to write what I wish," she said in a soft voice. "Will you do me the favor of coming here for fifteen days?"

"Yes!" Bernadette replied.

"I do not promise to make you happy in this world, but in the next," the Lady concluded.

Bernadette returned to the grotto the next day, accompanied by her mother and her Aunt Bernarde. Again the Lady came. The scene was repeated the next day, Saturday, with about thirty of the townspeople coming to watch. The following day, Sunday, February 21, the Lady appeared to Bernadette for the sixth time. Now the crowd of curious spectators had grown to 100.

That very afternoon, Bernadette was taken to Police Commissioner Jacomet's office for questioning. The town officials were getting nervous about the strange events and the growing crowds at Massabielle.

Commissioner Jacomet intended to prove that the whole thing was a hoax. He tried in every way to confuse Bernadette in his questioning, but she calmly corrected him point by point.

"So, this lady was dressed in a blue dress with a white sash," repeated Jacomet.

"No, Sir. It was a white dress with a blue sash."

"And she was about nineteen or twenty years old?"

"No, as I've told you, she was about seventeen."

The interrogation dragged on for an hour.

"You've twisted everything I've told you," Bernadette cried.

"I'm only reading back to you what you said," Jacomet retorted, his face flushed with rage.

"No, sir!"

"Yes!"

"No!"

"Yes!"

"No!"

Finally, Mr. Soubirous arrived to take

Bernadette back home, but only after Jacomet had threatened to lock her up.

Once again Bernadette's parents forbade her to go to the grotto. But on February 22, her desire to return grew so strong that she disobeyed their orders and went anyway. The Lady did not appear. The next day, the 23rd, Mr. and Mrs. Soubirous reluctantly gave in and allowed Bernadette to go to Massabielle. There she again met the Lady. In the visits that followed, the beautiful Lady asked Bernadette to do penance, to pray to God for the conversion of sinners and to drink from and wash in the spring. But there was no spring of water at Massabielle. This is why the 300 spectators who had gathered at the grotto on February 25 believed that Bernadette had gone mad when they saw her frantically scraping the earth with her bare hands. What the people couldn't see was the tiny trickle of water that had appeared at the bottom of the hole she had scooped out. In obedience to the Lady, Bernadette washed her face with this muddy mixture and then drank it. Most of the crowd turned away in disgust. But later that day some curious persons discovered the trickle of water and began to enlarge the small hole Bernadette had made. The water continued to flow and increase. It soon became clear and clean.

On March 2, during her thirteenth visit to the grotto, the beautiful young Lady made a request. "Tell the priests that I desire to have a chapel built here and that people are to come here in procession."

Bernadette obediently went to her pastor, Father Peyramale, with this message. A beautiful Lady, whom no one else could see, appearing in the rocks of a cliff and now asking for a chapel and processions…. This was all too much for the priest.

"And what's this Lady's name?" Father Peyramale bellowed.

"I don't know," Bernadette honestly replied.

"Well you'll have to ask her," the priest said roughly. "Tell her the pastor of Lourdes needs to know her name."

At the Lady's next visit, Bernadette asked her name. The young Lady only smiled and repeated her request for a chapel.

Bernadette reported this back to Father Peyramale. "If your Lady wants a chapel, she must give us a sign," he decided. "Ask her to make the rosebush at the grotto suddenly bloom—now in March—in front of everyone. If she does this, we'll have her chapel built."

On March 25, the feast of the Annunciation, Bernadette again asked the Lady, four times, Father Peyramale's important question, "What is your name?" At Bernadette's fourth try, a change came over the beautiful Lady. She seemed to be praying. She stretched out both arms toward the earth then raised and folded her hands, looking up toward heaven. "I am the Immaculate Conception," she said. And then she was gone.

This was a very strange name. So as not to forget it, Bernadette repeated it over and over again all the way to the priests' house.

Pushing open the door and walking straight up to Father Peyramale, Bernadette nearly shouted, "I am the Immaculate Conception."

"Do you know what these words mean?" the pastor asked in a trembling voice.

"No, Father," Bernadette admitted.

"All right, then go home now," Father Peyramale said quietly.

Bernadette was confused. Later that afternoon she asked a neighbor what "Immaculate Conception" meant.

"Immaculate Conception is the name we give to the privilege God gave Mary when he preserved her from sin from the very beginning of her existence," the woman explained. "God kept Mary from all sin and filled her with his grace because she was to become the Mother of his Son."

It was then that Bernadette realized that her Lady was really the Blessed Virgin Mary!

Mary appeared to Bernadette for the last time on July 16, 1858. Several years later, Bernadette entered the convent of the Sisters of Charity of Nevers. She died there at the age of thirty-five, after having lived a quiet life of love and service to her sisters. Bernadette was named a saint on December 8, 1933—the feast of the Immaculate Conception.

Over one hundred years have passed since the Blessed Mother visited Bernadette eighteen times at the grotto of Lourdes. Millions of people have traveled to Lourdes to pray at the basilica that has been built there. The waters of the spring continue to flow and many miracles and graces have been received by the people who drink it or bathe in it with faith. The shrine at Lourdes continues to remind us of the message Mary brought to us through Bernadette: "Pray for yourselves and for people who sin against God. Change your hearts and live as Jesus taught you. Believe in God's love for you!"

We celebrate the feast of Our Lady of Lourdes every year on February 11.

Our Lady of Lourdes, pray for us!

6

OUR LADY OF KNOCK

Knock, a quaint little village of County Mayo in the west of Ireland, was very poor. Its people were poor. Its homes were poor. Its church was poor. Poverty seemed to be its very way of life.

In 1878, a great storm severely damaged the village Church of Saint John the Baptist. A good part of the roof was ruined, the windows were broken, and the three statues that graced the simple church were smashed by the wind and water.

Poor, but proud, the villagers scraped together every penny they could, and their pastor, Father Cavanagh, immediately ordered two new statues.

The people swept. They cleaned. They polished. Soon their tiny church was repaired and restored. All of this happened just about a year before the extraordinary event that was to change the village of Knock forever....

It was August 21, 1879. A light mist had turned into a soft drizzle. Clouds had lowered and the skies had darkened. By 7:00 P.M., heavy rains were pounding the remote village. The downpour was so sudden and steady that farmers and field workers were forced to abandon their chores and scurry home for shelter.

Mary McLoughlin, Father Cavanagh's housekeeper, glanced at the old clock hanging on the wall.

"I'd better be getting back to the rectory," she announced to her friend Margaret Beirne. "It's getting late."

As the housekeeper swung her cape over her shoulders, Mary Beirne, Margaret's eldest daughter, peered out the window. "I'll walk back with you," she offered. "It's raining so hard. I don't want you to go back alone."

"Mary Beirne!" Mary McLoughlin chuckled. "Then who will walk back with *you?*"

The three women laughed. "Never you mind," Margaret broke in. "The rain can't last long. Now under the umbrellas with you."

And so, arm in arm, the two Marys set off for the rectory on the hill.

As they got close, Mary Beirne noticed something unusual. "Look," she nudged the housekeeper. "Look at those three statues over there."

"I did notice them on my way to your mother's," Mary McLoughlin admitted, "but I didn't pay much attention."

"What in the world are they doing out in the rain?" Mary Beirne wondered aloud.

The curious women stopped in their tracks, with the rain thumping hard on their umbrellas. The same thoughts were running through their minds. *Why would Father Cavanagh have bought more statues? We just got new ones last year. Besides, everyone knows the parish could never afford statues as beautiful as these...and Father Cavanagh, he doesn't have the money. He's already pawned his watch and sold his horse to help the poor....*

Yet, there they were! Three of the most stunning statues the women had ever seen!

"Let's get closer," Mary Beirne suggested, "and have a better look."

The two approached the lovely statues, completely forgetting the wind and rain that pelted them from all sides.

"There's a light coming from the figures," Mary Beirne observed.

"I don't understand this at all," Mary McLoughlin replied, shaking her head.

"Look there! The light is getting brighter!"

"What does it mean?" the housekeeper questioned nervously.

"Mary…Mary…they're not statues at all. They can't be…. They're *moving!* And that one, to be sure, is the Blessed Mother!" exclaimed Mary Beirne.

Both women were left speechless. Neither moved. Mary Beirne was the first to regain her composure. "I've never seen such a magnificent sight in all my life!" she whispered with emotion.

"Nor I, Mary, nor I," the housekeeper stammered, clasping her hands tightly.

The three figures seemed to hover above the tall, uncut grass, while the front wall of the church served as their backdrop.

"Truly they're *not* statues," Mary Beirne repeated.

"No. They can't be," Mary McLoughlin agreed. "Their feet barely touch the tips of the blades of grass…and look, the ground beneath them is perfectly dry!"

"Yes, I'm sure that's the Blessed Mother in the middle," Mary Beirne insisted. "Look at how her hands are raised and her eyes are lifted up to heaven. She must be praying."

"That's the Blessed Mother in the middle, with St. Joseph on her right and St. John on her left."

"And that must be Saint Joseph on her right," pointed out the housekeeper.

"The figure on the left looks very much like Saint John the Evangelist. I've seen his statue in the church at Lecanvey," Mary Beirne added.

Behind and slightly to the side of the three figures stood an altar topped by a large cross. Standing on the altar was a lamb, symbolizing Jesus, the Lamb of God.

The women were no longer afraid. They were thrilled. "Quick! Go call your family, Mary!" the housekeeper cried. "I'll wait here."

Mary Beirne rushed home. Pushing open the door of her house she breathlessly announced, "There's a vision in front of the church wall...under the gable! Come...quickly!"

"A what?" her brother Dominick asked.

"A vision! A vision!" Mary shouted.

"Don't be ridiculous," he sarcastically retorted. "It's probably just a reflection of some sort."

"Wait, Dominick," Mrs. Beirne intervened. "Let's listen to her. Look at her face. Surely she's seen *something!*"

"It was no reflection," Mary pleaded. "We have no statue of Saint John in the church, and our Blessed Mother statue doesn't show Mary with her arms and eyes raised to heaven. Please, come back with me, Dominick!"

"You've had some kind of hallucination," her brother replied coldly. "And you'd better stop this nonsense before you make a spectacle of yourself. The whole village will be laughing at you."

"Mary, where is this vision?" her mother asked.

"Atop the tall grass, before the front of the church, under the gable."

"Let's go with her," Mrs. Beirne said, taking her granddaughter Catherine by the hand.

"In the pouring rain?" Dominick objected.

"Yes!" his mother insisted.

The four arrived at the church drenched and chilled.

Dominick pushed his way to the front. "I want to be the first to see this vision," he said mockingly.

Suddenly the color drained from his face. "It's true!" he whispered. "It's all true!"

Word travels quickly in a small village and before long there were eighteen spectators at the site. The youngest was a six-year-old-child, the oldest a seventy-five-year-old man. The rain continued to pour down on the kneeling villagers, but it never touched the three figures or the grass and ground beneath them.

"Gaze upon the crown of the Blessed Virgin, will you!" an onlooker called out.

"Yes, yes, it's lined with glittering crosses. And look at the beautiful rose at the point where the crown touches her brow!"

"She's never once looked down on us or spoken to us," said another.

"It's because she's praying," someone else interrupted. "The Blessed Mother has come not to tell us, but to *show* us what we must do."

Around 11:00 P.M., an elderly woman was so overwhelmed by the vision that she rushed to embrace the Blessed Virgin's feet. Her arms passed through empty air. "But where is she?" the old woman asked in bewilderment. "I see her, but I can't feel her!"

She dropped to her knees before the vision. "The ground under the figures is completely dry!" she murmured. "It's been raining steadily for hours. How can it be?"

"Everything is possible with God," an old man quietly replied. "Everything."

Not long after, the silent figures vanished.

Since that memorable night so many years ago, countless pilgrims have journeyed to the shrine of Our Lady of Knock, on the hill now called Mary's Hill. A basilica has been built and miraculous cures have taken place at the site. The feast of Our Lady of Knock is celebrated there annually on August 21.

Today over one million people visit Knock each year. They come to fulfill the Blessed Mother's silent request, "Pray!"

Our Lady of Knock, pray for us!

7

OUR LADY OF FATIMA

It was a beautiful spring day in 1916. Three young Portuguese shepherds were pasturing their small flock of sheep on the slopes of a hill called the Cabeço, just outside the village of Fatima.

Francisco Marto was eight. His sister, Jacinta, was six. Lucia dos Santos, their nine-year-old cousin, completed the trio.

The children had eaten their lunch in a small cave and prayed a quick rosary. (Following their "method," this rosary was very short. Instead of saying the complete prayers, one of the three would call out "Hail Mary!" and the other two would answer "Holy Mary!" They would end each decade with the simple words "Our Father.") Just as they started a game, a strong gust of wind rattled the trees. Looking up in surprise, the children saw a white figure hovering in mid-air above the nearby olive orchard.

The mysterious figure began moving toward them! The young shepherds stood frozen to the spot, not knowing what to do. As it came closer, the children could see that its features were those of a handsome young teenage boy, about fifteen years old.

"Do not be afraid," he said. "I am the Angel of Peace. Pray with me." Then the angel knelt, bowing his head to the ground. The children followed his example and fell to their knees. They repeated after the angel this prayer: "My God, I believe, I adore, I hope and I love you! I beg pardon for those who do not believe, do not adore, do not hope and do not love you."

After praying this way with the children three times, the angel rose. "Pray like this," he instructed. "The hearts of Jesus and Mary are prepared to listen to your prayers." Then he was gone. The children were so overwhelmed by what had happened that they remained there for a long time, repeating the prayer over and over again. They told no one about the mysterious experience.

Summer came. One day, Jacinta, Francisco, and Lucia were playing in the shade of the well in Lucia's yard. Suddenly the same angel was there with them. "What are you doing?" he kindly asked. "Pray, pray much. The Hearts of Jesus and Mary have wonderful plans for you…. Offer prayers and sacrifices to the Most High."

"How?" asked Lucia.

"In every way you can, offer a sacrifice as an act of reparation for the many sins which offend God and as a prayer for the conversion of sinners. In this way you will bring peace to your country. I am the Guardian Angel of Portugal. Above all, accept and bear with patience the sufferings which the Lord will send you."

The children knelt with their foreheads touching the ground. They remained praying in this way for a long time.

Two or three months later, the angel visited the young shepherds once again. This time he came holding a chalice. Above it he held a white Host from which drops of Blood were falling into the chalice.

Leaving the Host and chalice suspended in the air, the angel knelt and bowed his head to the ground. He invited the children to follow his example. Then he prayed three times: "O Most Holy Trinity, Father, Son, and Holy Spirit, I adore you profoundly. I offer you the most precious Body, Blood, soul and divinity of Jesus Christ, present in all the tabernacles of the world, in reparation for the outrages, sacrileges and indifference by which he is offended. By the infinite merits of the Sacred Heart of Jesus, and of the Immaculate Heart of Mary, I beg the conversion of poor sinners."

The angel then stood and gave the Host to Lucia. Next he allowed Jacinta and Francisco to drink from the chalice.

"Take," he said, "the Body and Blood of Jesus horribly insulted by ungrateful people. Make reparation for their crimes. Console your God."

The angel knelt with his head to the ground again, repeated the Most Holy Trinity prayer three more times with the shepherds, and then disappeared. The children never saw him again.

After Mass on Sunday, May 13, 1917, the three children decided to pasture their sheep at the Cova da Iria, a valley where Lucia's parents owned a small plot of land.

After lunch, the young shepherds knelt to pray the rosary. Then they continued with some of their usual games.

It was a beautiful, clear day and the sun was shining brightly. Suddenly a bolt of lightning streaked across the sky.

"A storm could be coming," observed Lucia. "I think we should go home."

Her younger cousins agreed, and within minutes the three had rounded up the sheep and were hurrying down the hillside. Another flash of lightning cut across their path. Frightened, the children started to run. But when they reached the bottom of the valley, they stopped, and found they couldn't go on. Just steps away from them was the most beautiful young Lady they had ever seen! She was standing upon a small green holm oak tree (a tree whose leaves look like the holly plant) and was enveloped in a light more brilliant than the sun. "Do not be afraid," the Lady said. "I will not hurt you."

The Lady, who was looking down at the children, seemed to be between fifteen and eighteen years old. She wore a long white dress, drawn at the neck with a golden cord. A white mantle edged in gold covered her head. In her hands she held a white rosary with a silver cross.

The children stared in awe. Finally, Lucia found the courage to speak. "Where do you come from?" she asked.

"I come from heaven," the Lady replied.

"And why have you come here?"

"I have come to ask you children to meet me here at this same hour on the thirteenth of every month, for six months in a row, until October. Then I will tell you who I am and what I wish."

"Will I go to heaven?" Lucia asked, beginning to feel more comfortable with the Lady.

"Yes," came the answer.

"And Jacinta?"

"Jacinta too."

"And Francisco?"

The Lady turned to look at Francisco. "Yes, certainly he too will come. But first he will have to pray many, many rosaries."

Lucia asked a few more questions. Then it was the young Lady's turn to ask a question: "Will you offer yourselves to God, ready to make sacrifices and to accept willingly all the sufferings he will send you, in order to make reparation for the sins with which the Divine Majesty is offended and to obtain the conversion of sinners?"

"Yes, we want to!" Lucia answered in the name of all three.

The Lady gave them a beautiful smile. "You will have to suffer much," she added, "but the grace of God will assist and comfort you always."

Then, opening her hands, which had been joined, she let a ray of mysterious light fall upon the children. It seemed to enter their hearts and souls. Somehow they understood that the light was God. They felt that God was embracing them. They fell to their knees. In their hearts they heard the words of this prayer, which they lovingly repeated: *Most Holy Trinity, I adore you! My God, my God, I love you in the Most Blessed Sacrament!*

The Lady had one last recommendation: "Say the rosary every day, to obtain peace for the world." Then she silently rose from the treetop and glided off toward the east. The children watched in amazement as she slowly faded away.

Lucia thought it best for them not to tell anyone of what they had seen. But that night, Jacinta told her parents. This was the beginning of the suffering that the Lady had predicted. Word got out to the village. The children were laughed at and interrogated, threatened and punished. But they never changed their story. And they insisted that they had to go back to the Cova da Iria on the thirteenth of every month.

June 13 found them kneeling at the Cova praying their rosary. About fifty curious people had come to watch. Suddenly the children saw lightning. They ran to the three-foot holm oak. Yes, the Lady was there!

"What do you wish?" Lucia asked.

"I wish you to come here on the thirteenth of next month and to recite the rosary every day. After each one of the mysteries, my children, I want you to pray like this: *O my Jesus, forgive us our sins, save us from the fires of hell. Lead all souls to heaven, especially those most in need of your mercy.* I also want you to learn how to read and write. Later I will tell you what else I desire."

Next the Lady told Lucia that she would come to take Jacinta and Francisco to heaven very soon, but that Lucia would have to stay on earth for a long while.

The Lady again appeared to the children on July 13, 1917. She asked them to continue to come to the Cova every thirteenth of the month and promised that she would reveal her name and work a miracle in October. "Sacrifice yourselves for sinners," the beautiful Lady advised, "and say often, but especially when making a sacrifice, *O my Jesus, it is for love of you, in reparation for the offenses committed against the Immaculate Heart of Mary, and for the conversion of sinners.*"

At that point, the Lady revealed to the children a three-part secret. Lucia, who was afterward given permission by God and the Blessed Mother to reveal the secret, did reveal it many years later, at two different times. Now we know that the first part of the secret consisted in a vision of hell, which the Lady allowed the three children to see. "You have seen hell, where the souls of poor, unrepentant sinners go," the Lady explained. "To save them, God wants to establish in the world devotion to my Immaculate Heart. If what I tell you will be done, many souls will be saved and there will be peace. But if it is not done, if people do not stop offending God, God's justice will show itself with new and more serious punishments."

The second part of the secret had to do with a prediction of World War II. At that time, World War I was raging. On that July 13, 1917, the Lady told the children that the war would end, but that it would be followed by an even worse war if people did not stop offending God. This prediction came true and World War II brought terrible suffering to countless people from 1939 to 1945.

"I come to ask that Russia be consecrated to my Immaculate Heart," the Lady told the children, "and that Holy Communion be received in reparation on the first Saturday of every month. If my wishes are fulfilled, I promise that Russia will be converted and there will be peace.

"If the people do not do as I ask, Russia will spread her errors throughout the world, starting wars and persecutions against the Church. Many good people will be martyred, and the Holy Father will have much to suffer. Many nations will be destroyed. In the end, my Immaculate Heart will triumph. The Holy Father will consecrate Russia to me and she will be converted, and a period of peace will be granted the world."

In the third part of the secret, the children saw an angel, holding a flaming sword, appear to the left of the Lady. But the flames died out when they came into contact with the brilliance radiating from the Lady. The angel pointed to the earth and cried out, "Penance! Penance! Penance!" Then the children saw a bishop dressed in white, whom they understood to be the Pope, climbing up a steep mountain. He was followed by other bishops, priests, religious, and lay people.

Before they got to the top of the mountain, on which was a big cross, they had to pass through a ruined city. The Pope was suffering very much to see all the destruction. Many people had died, and the Pope was praying for their souls as he continued to climb. At the top of the mountain, the Pope knelt at the foot of the large cross. There he was shot at and killed by soldiers. The soldiers also killed all those who had followed the Pope up the mountain. But beneath the cross two angels gathered up the blood of these martyrs and sprinkled it on the souls who were making their way to God.

We can interpret the secret given to the children as referring to things that have already happened in the twentieth century, especially the wars and the suffering of the Popes and all those who have tried to live and preach Jesus' Gospel to a world that is opposed to it. The meaning of the secret is that God and the Blessed Mother wish us to pray and do penance for ourselves and for others so that all people may stop offending God and begin to live the way Jesus came to teach us to live—in love and mercy.

Jacinta, Francisco and Lucia were supposed to meet the Lady at the Cova again on August 13. But the mayor of the nearby town of Ourem had taken them into custody. He questioned them for hours. The children told him what they could, but refused to reveal the secret. The enraged mayor had them locked up overnight. The next day, he had them sent to the town prison, where they spent another night. The following morning, the mayor called them back to his office, threatening to boil them in oil if they still refused to "cooperate" and tell him the secret. All three insisted that the Blessed Virgin had commanded them not to tell it to anyone. The mayor finally gave up and drove them back to Fatima.

Although the children had been forced to miss their August 13 appointment with the beautiful Lady, she appeared to them on the nineteenth as they were tending their sheep at a place called Valinhos. "Pray. Pray much," she told them. "Many souls go to hell because no one makes sacrifices for them."

On September 13, a crowd of about 30,000 had gathered at the Cova da Iria in expectation of the next apparition. Mary appeared, urging the children to continue praying the rosary for the war to end. She also promised to bring the Infant Jesus and Saint Joseph with her the next month.

On October 13, the last day of the promised apparitions, nearly 70,000 people waited in the pouring rain and thick mud for the Blessed Virgin to appear to the shepherds. Jacinta, Francisco and Lucia arrived at the Cova around noon. They began praying the rosary. Soon the Lady appeared.

"Who are you and what do you wish?" Lucia asked.

The radiant Lady answered, "I am the Lady of the Rosary. I desire that a chapel be built on this spot in my honor. Continue always to pray the rosary every day. I promise that if people will change their lives, I will hear their prayers, and will bring the war to a speedy end…. I have come to tell people to ask forgiveness for their sins." The Virgin Mary's face appeared very sad as she added, "Do not offend the Lord our God anymore, because he is already so much offended." Then she pointed up to heaven.

Turning to see what the Lady was pointing at, Lucia suddenly cried out, "Look at the sun!"

The rain had abruptly stopped and the sun had appeared. But instead of its usual blinding brilliance, it was a cool, silvery-white color. The people were able to look directly into it without hurting their eyes. As the crowd watched, the sun began to spin like an enormous wheel of fire, shooting out spectacular shafts of every color imaginable. Upturned faces, trees, the countryside, everything was fantastically colored by its rays. Twice for a brief moment, the sun stopped. Then the violent swirling and swerving began all over again, raining down brighter and brighter colors.

In the meantime, the children alone saw four scenes, one after the other, beside the sun. First Saint Joseph, holding the Infant Jesus, joined the Blessed Mother there. Then Jesus, as a grown man stood at the base of the sun and blessed the people. Next Mary appeared as Our Lady of Sorrows. Finally Mary appeared as Our Lady of Mount Carmel, holding the brown scapular in her hand.

Then, without warning, the sun began a mad plunge toward the earth. The people screamed in terror. Many believed it was the end of the world.

"Have mercy on us, Lord!"

"Mary, help us!" the onlookers cried as they fell to their knees all over the muddy field.

Just as it seemed ready to hit the earth, the silver ball abruptly halted and stopped spinning. Slowly, majestically, it rose higher and higher until it was safely locked once again in the heavens. There it regained its normal brilliance.

When the people had recovered their senses, they realized that their clothes, which had been drenched in the torrential downpour, were perfectly dry.

"A miracle! A miracle!" the shout went up.

As the Blessed Mother had promised, she soon came to take both Francisco and Jacinta home to heaven. Both caught a severe form of the flu that was sweeping Europe at the time. Francisco died on April 4, 1919. He was almost eleven years old. Jacinta died on February 20, 1920. She was nine, going on ten. Both Jacinta and Francisco were beatified by Pope John Paul II in Fatima on May 13, 2000. They are the youngest children the Church has ever honored as "blesseds."

As of this writing, Lucia is still living as a Carmelite nun in Coimbra, Portugal. She's over ninety years old. As the Blessed Virgin had predicted, Lucia was to stay a long while on earth, spreading devotion to the Immaculate Heart of Mary.

The Cova da Iria is now a shrine which two million pilgrims visit each year. Here

God's people feel especially close to Mary and ponder her message: "Pray the rosary for peace! Ask forgiveness for your sins. Do not offend the Lord any longer."

We celebrate the feast of Our Lady of Fatima each year on October 13.

Our Lady of Fatima, pray for us!

8

OUR LADY OF BEAURAING

Jesus always loved children. In fact, in the Gospels we read that he told his disciples, "Let the little children come to me...." And so it's not surprising that Jesus often granted children the rarest of privileges—encounters with his own Mother!

Beauraing, a small farming village in Belgium, was the site of another of these special meetings in 1932.

Gilberte Voisin was thirteen years old. Her sister, Fernande, was fifteen, and their mischievous brother Albert was eleven.

Their two close friends were fourteen-year-old Andrée Degeimbre and her nine-year-old sister, also named Gilberte.

On November 29, 1932, Fernande and Albert, Andrée and her sister Gilberte, went to the convent school to pick up Gilberte Voisin and walk her home. (Gilberte was a semi-boarder. She stayed at school for a study period and a meal after regular classes were over, leaving for home at about 6:30 P.M. each evening.) Arriving at the convent, the children opened the gate to the yard and started up the gravel path to the front door. They rang the doorbell and waited impatiently for a sister to answer.

All of a sudden, they were startled by Albert's cry. "Look! Look over there! The Blessed Virgin is walking above the railroad bridge! Do you see her? She's dressed all in white!"

Albert was known for playing jokes and tricks. Just that evening he had rung five doorbells on the way to the convent. But there was something about his facial expression that told the girls he wasn't joking this time. They followed his pointing finger.

"Oh!" one of the girls gasped. "There *is* a Lady in white on the bridge!"

"And she *does* look like she's walking in the air...."

Frightened, the children pounded harder on the convent door.

"What on earth is the matter?" Sister Valeria demanded as she finally pulled it open.

"Look, Sister! Over there—it's the Blessed Mother!" the children exclaimed, pointing to the railway bridge that arched over the street about fifty yards from where they stood.

The sister stared, but saw nothing. She went back in to call Gilberte Voisin. As Gilberte stepped outside, she cried, "There's a Lady in white over there! She seems to be floating!"

Uneasy and confused, and not knowing what else to do, Sister Valeria said goodnight to the children. Leaving the convent yard, they ran to the Degeimbre house. Mrs. Degeimbre, a widow, didn't believe them. Gilberte, Fernande and Albert then continued on to their home. Mr. and Mrs. Voisin, who were no longer practicing their Catholic faith, also refused to believe them. "Children's fantasies," Mrs. Voisin smiled to her husband.

The next evening, the Voisin and Degeimbre children again set out to meet Gilberte at the school. The five were heading out of the convent yard when they again saw the Lady walking over the railway bridge. Once more they ran into the Degeimbre house, shouting, "We've seen the Lady again! And she *is* the Blessed Mother!"

Mrs. Degeimbre became very upset. "Someone's playing a trick on you!" she warned.

"Oh no!" the children insisted. "We've

seen her! And she's much more beautiful that her statues!"

"I'll put an end to this nonsense!" the annoyed mother promised.

The next evening, December 1, Mrs. Degeimbre, along with a group of friends and neighbors, followed her two daughters and Albert and Fernande Voisin to the convent. She was wielding a heavy stick.

"There she is! There she is!" the children cried. "She's come closer!"

"Yes! She's in the garden now!"

The Lady had appeared for a moment on the garden pathway and then vanished.

Mrs. Degeimbre, who had seen nothing, sent the children to call Gilberte Voisin. Meanwhile, she beat the shrubs with her stick, hoping to force the trickster out. The other adults joined in the search.

Then Gilberte emerged from the convent.

"Oh, oh, look!" Mrs. Degeimbre heard. She turned, the stick clutched tightly in her nervous hand.

"The Lady was near the Lourdes grotto. She looked at us. She smiled at us," Gilberte announced.

"And where is she now?" Mrs. Degeimbre shrilly cried.

"She's gone."

"Gone? Of course…because she was never there!" Mrs. Degeimbre screeched.

"There she is again!" the children shouted excitedly. "Coming from the shrubs between the gate and the grotto!"

"Come out! Come out!" Mrs. Degeimbre screamed, frantically thrashing the bushes with her stick. But the Lady ascended toward heaven and disappeared.

At this point, little Gilberte Degeimbre was so overcome by the beauty of the Blessed Mother that she felt weak and had to be taken home. Gilberte Voisin stayed with her. Meanwhile, the other three children returned to the convent accompanied by Mrs. Degeimbre, and Mr. and Mrs. Voisin.

Before reaching the gate of the convent yard, the children shouted, "There she is!" and immediately fell to their knees as if they had been struck down. With unusually high-pitched voices, they began to pray in unison, "Hail Mary, full of grace…."

The Lady was now beneath a hawthorn tree in the convent garden. She seemed to be between eighteen to twenty years old and wore a pleated white gown without a belt and a white veil. Rays surrounded her head,

"There she is!" the children shouted
as they fell to their knees.

forming what looked like a crown of sunshine. A kind of blue light shimmered from her whole person. She held her hands together as if she were praying, separating them just before she disappeared.

This was the sixth apparition the children had seen. Twenty-seven more would follow in which the Blessed Virgin would always appear by the hawthorn tree and the children would always immediately fall to their knees and pray in an uncommonly high tone of voice.

The next day, December 2, Mother Theophile, the superior of the convent, took matters into her own hands. She had the garden gates locked and two ferocious dogs stationed in the yard. But the children returned anyway. Kneeling on the cobblestones outside the garden, they again saw the Blessed Virgin.

"Are you the Immaculate Virgin?" Albert asked.

The beautiful Lady smiled and nodded yes.

"What do you want?"

"Always be good," came the Blessed Mother's reply. These were the first words she had spoken to the children.

Mother Theophile forbade the children

to return the next day, December 3. When she saw that they obeyed, she relented and allowed them to come again after that.

By now word had spread throughout Beauraing and beyond. Crowds began to gather at the convent yard each evening. When the Blessed Mother appeared on December 6, she held a rosary for the first time.

On December 8, the feast of the Immaculate Conception, about 15,000 people crowded the area of the convent garden, hoping to see a miracle. The children knelt with their eyes fixed on the same point. They faces were radiant with joy. Some doctors had come to observe them. One of these held a burning match under Gilberte Voisin's left hand, but the girl noticed nothing and experienced neither pain nor burn marks afterward. Other doctors pinched and pricked the five children. They shone high intensity flashlights into their eyes. But the children heard, felt and saw nothing of what was happening around them.

After this, the Blessed Virgin no longer came every evening and the children now had to wait for her. On December 17, Mary asked that a chapel be built on the site of the apparitions. On December 21, she told the children, "I am the Immaculate Virgin." On

December 23, Fernande asked her, "Why do you come here?"

The Virgin answered, "So that people will come here on pilgrimage."

While all five children saw Mary on the night of December 29, only Fernande saw a vision of her Immaculate Heart. It appeared to be golden with brilliant rays pouring from it. The next day, Gilberte Voisin and Andrée also saw the heart, and the Blessed Mother told Fernande, "Pray. Pray very much."

On December 31, Mary was silent, but all five children saw her heart.

On January 1, the Lady told Gilberte Voisin to "Pray always." On January 2, she explained that she would speak to each of them separately on the following day.

January 3, 1933 was the beautiful Lady's final appearance to the children. Between 30,000–35,000 people crowded the area around the convent. Our Lady revealed individual secrets to all of the children except Fernande, who neither saw nor heard Mary with the others. "I will convert sinners," Mary promised. "I am the Mother of God, the Queen of Heaven. Pray all the time."

Fernande knelt in tears after the Lady had disappeared and the other children had been taken into the convent to be questioned.

Suddenly there was a loud clap of thunder. A ball of fire appeared on the hawthorn tree. The lingering crowd heard the sound and saw the fire.

The Blessed Mother had returned to pay Fernande a special visit.

"Do you love my Son?" Mary asked.

"Oh, yes, yes I do!" Fernande exclaimed.

"Do you love me?"

"Yes, yes!"

"Then sacrifice yourself for me." At this point the Blessed Virgin extended her arms in a gesture of farewell, again showing Fernande her heart which radiated love and light. "Goodbye." And she was gone.

Mr. and Mrs. Voisin were among the first to return to the practice of their faith after the visions at Beauraing.

On August 22, 1946, a large statue representing Mary as she appeared to the children was erected under the hawthorn tree. On August 21, 1954, a chapel was blessed at the same site. A new basilica was also opened in 1968.

Andrée and Fernande have died, but as of 1999, the other three visionaries were still living.

Today, about one million pilgrims annually visit the shrine at Beauraing, fulfilling Mary's request for prayer. August 22 is celebrated there as the feast of the Immaculate Heart of Mary, the official Beauraing feast.

Our Lady of Beauraing, Virgin of the Golden Heart, pray for us!

OUR LADY OF BANNEUX

It was winter in Banneux, Belgium, a poor, tiny hamlet with a population of less than 500. The soft snow covering the pine trees by Mariette Beco's house had turned to ice.

On the evening of Sunday, January 15, 1933, twelve days after the Marian apparitions at Beauraing had ended, Mariette knelt peering out the window. *Where's Julien?* she wondered. *It's 7:00 P.M. He should be home by now.* As the eldest in her large family (she was nearly twelve) Mariette was responsible for helping to care for her younger brothers and sisters. And tonight her brother Julien was late in returning home.

Continuing to gaze into the darkness, Mariette noticed a light hovering in the front yard. She suddenly realized that the light was actually the form of a smiling young Lady, a Lady who was looking in her direction! The Lady's head was tilted toward her left shoulder and her hands were joined in prayer.

"Mama, there's a Lady in the yard!" Mariette called excitedly.

"Don't talk nonsense," her mother wearily replied.

"She's lovely! Dressed in a white gown with a sky blue sash," Mariette continued. "And she's as bright as light."

"Maybe it's the Blessed Virgin," Mrs. Beco laughingly teased.

"Come see for yourself, Mama!"

To put an end to the whole thing, Mrs. Beco went to the window. She was astonished to see a white light, and what appeared to be the form of a person, but nothing was clear.

"It's a witch!" her mother declared, dropping back the sheet that served as a curtain.

"No! No! It really *is* the Blessed Mother," Mariette insisted. "She's praying. I can see her lips moving." Mariette pulled out her rosary and began to pray herself. After several minutes, she cried out, "She's calling me to come to her!"

Mariette rushed toward the door, but her mother intercepted her and locked it. "Have you lost your mind? You will *not* go out there!"

The disappointed girl returned to the window. The Lady was gone.

The next day at school, Mariette told the story to her best friend Josephine Léonard.

Josephine burst out laughing. But when Mariette began to sob, the girl realized that this was no joke. "We should go tell Father Jamin," she said decisively.

The twenty-nine-year-old pastor dismissed the story, thinking that Mariette had heard of the apparitions in Beauraing. He was astonished, though, when Mariette began faithfully attending morning Mass and religious education, after having neglected both for several months. After Wednesday morning's class, the priest brought her into the church. He tried to get her to agree that what she *thought* she saw was the statue of Our Lady of Lourdes.

"No. I know what I saw," Mariette insisted. "The Blessed Virgin was different from this statue...and so much more beautiful!"

At 7:00 P.M. on Wednesday, January 18, Mariette darted out into the yard. Her father followed her. The girl saw the radiant Lady descend from the tops of two tall pine trees. Mariette fell to her knees and began praying the rosary. The Virgin, suspended about fifteen inches above the ground on a small cloud, came to rest five feet in front of Mariette. A white rosary hung from her right arm.

Mr. Beco, who saw nothing, tried to distract his daughter, going back to the house and slamming the door loudly. But Mariette heard nothing. He finally shouted into the darkness, "You've gone crazy!" before leaving on his bicycle to call Father Jamin to the scene. The pastor wasn't home, and Mr. Beco returned instead with a neighbor and his son, just in time to see Mariette walking down the road, as if she were following someone. "Where are you going, Mariette?" her father desperately cried. "Come back!"

"She's calling me to follow her!" Mariette replied without turning around or stopping.

The Lady led Mariette to a spring that no one knew existed. "Put your hands in the water," the Blessed Virgin instructed the girl. "This stream is reserved for me." Then she was gone.

Mr. Beco was not a religious man. But these strange events greatly impressed him.

For the first time since his boyhood, he felt the need for God. The next day, he asked Father Jamin to hear his confession and to give him Communion.

At 7:00 P.M. on January 19, Mariette threw a shawl over her shoulders and went out to the front yard accompanied by her father. Eleven other people had come to watch. Mariette knelt in the snow and began praying the rosary.

"She's here!" the girl soon shouted with joy. "Who are you?" Mariette asked the Lady.

"I am the Virgin of the Poor," the Lady lovingly answered.

Once more, the Blessed Virgin led Mariette to the spring, telling her, "This spring is reserved for all nations—to relieve the sick."

Mariette again saw the Lady in the front yard on Friday, January 20. "What do you wish?" she asked her.

"A small chapel," the Blessed Virgin replied. Before leaving, the Virgin laid her hands on Mariette and then with her right hand, traced the sign of the cross over her. At this point, Mariette fainted. But she soon recovered and was found to be perfectly normal by a doctor who examined her.

Mariette continued to go out to the yard every evening, but it was three weeks before Mary came again. During this time her classmates in catechism class made fun of her. Some called her Bernadette and even asked for her "blessing."

On the evening of February 11, the feast of Our Lady of Lourdes, the Blessed Mother appeared as Mariette was praying the rosary in the yard. Mariette followed her back to the spring. "I come to relieve suffering," the Virgin told her.

"Thank you, thank you," Mariette murmured.

"Blessed Virgin," Mariette confided during the sixth apparition on Wednesday, February 15, "Father Jamin told me to ask you for a sign."

In the moments that followed, tears flooded Mariette's eyes and she fell prostrate on the ground.

"Why are you crying?" her mother asked her.

"Because she's gone."

"Did she answer your question about the sign?"

"Yes. She said, 'Believe in me; I will believe in you. Pray much.'"

The Blessed Mother had also entrusted a

secret to Mariette, but the girl never revealed it to anyone.

A seventh apparition took place on February 20, although Mariette continued to wait for the Lady every night. Smiling, the Virgin Mary led Mariette to the spring. "My dear child, pray much," she told her.

On Thursday March 2, 1933, the Blessed Virgin appeared to Mariette Beco for the eighth and final time. It was raining heavily, but the downpour suddenly stopped when the Blessed Virgin arrived. Mary seemed sad. "I am the Mother of the Savior, Mother of God," she told Mariette. "Pray much. Good-bye, until we meet in God."

Many years have passed since the Blessed Mother's apparitions at Banneux. But water continues to flow from the spring there and miraculous cures have taken place. The chapel that Mary requested has been built at Banneux, and her feast is celebrated there every January 15. Hundreds of thousands of pilgrims visit the shrine each year.

Mariette Beco married and raised a family of her own. She always avoided publicity, seeing herself as the instrument the Blessed Virgin used to bring us her message: "Pray. Pray much!"

The Virgin of the Poor appeared to a poor child in a poor town and gave the world a treasure: a spring whose waters can heal the body, when this is God's will, and move the soul to prayer.

Our Lady of Banneux, Virgin of the Poor, pray for us!

PRAYER

Virgin Mary, Mother of God, you are also our heavenly Mother.

Thank you for having appeared on earth at different times and places. Your visits have reminded us all that the sure way to reach God is to live as your Son Jesus has taught us—in love and obedience to the Gospel.

You've also asked us to pray for ourselves and for the whole world. You've shown us that prayer can change everything! I want to pray, Blessed Mother. Please teach me how. Lead me to Jesus, and help me to bring him to others in whatever ways I can.

Holy Mary, Mother of God, pray for me! Amen.

Glossary

1. **Basilica**—a large church of special importance that is patterned after a type of ancient Roman building.

2. **Beatification**—the ceremony in which the Pope, in the name of the Catholic Church, declares that a person lived a life of Gospel holiness in a heroic way. This is done after the person's life and holiness have been carefully researched. Beatification is the second step in the process of naming a person a saint. Once a person has been beatified, he or she is called by the title "Blessed."

3. **Confessor**—a priest who is authorized to hear confessions and celebrate with a person the sacrament of Reconciliation.

4. **Crusades**—a series of battles fought by European Christians between the 11th and 13th centuries. Their purpose was to recover, or in some cases, defend Christian lands, especially the Holy Land, from Muslim rule. Christians who fought in these wars were called Crusaders.

5. **Hermit**—a person who lives alone, devoting himself or herself to prayer.

6. **Incorrupt**—not subject to destruction. To say that a person's body is incorrupt means that God has preserved it from the natural process of deterioration that usually takes place after death.

7. **Monastery**—the place where friars, monks or nuns live as a community, dedicating themselves to a life of prayer.

8. **Novitiate**—a special period of training and probation for those who are preparing to become religious sisters, brothers or priests. The actual building where this training takes place is also called the novitiate.

9. **Penance**—a prayer or action that a person says or does to express his or her sorrow for sin.

10. **Pilgrims**—persons who travel to a holy place to pray and to feel closer to God. The journey they make is called a pilgrimage.

11. **Postulant**—a person taking his or her first steps in religious life; a candidate.

12. **Prostrate**—to lie face down or to bow very low.

13. **Ravine**—a narrow, deep valley, especially one created by running water.

14. **Recourse**—a turning to someone for help.

15. **Reparation**—the act of making up for a wrong or an injury. During her various apparitions our Blessed Mother has often asked us to make reparation for our own sins and the sins of others.

16. **Sanctuary**—as used in this book, the area of a church that is closest to the altar.

17. **Saracens**—Muslims who originally lived in the desert, on the outskirts of the Roman Empire. They resisted Roman attempts to take over their lands, and, during the Middle Ages, they fought against the Christian Crusaders.

Who are the Daughters of St. Paul?

We are Catholic sisters. Our mission is to be like Saint Paul and tell everyone about Jesus! There are so many ways for people to communicate with each other. We want to use all of them so everyone will know how much God loves them. We do this by printing books (you're holding one!), making radio shows, singing, helping people at our bookstores, using the Internet, and in many other ways.

Visit our website at www.pauline.org